KEBABS
◆ ON THE GRILL ◆

Creative Cooking Library

By the Editors of Sunset Books

SUNSET BOOKS
President & Publisher: Susan J. Maruyama
Director, Finance & Business Affairs: Gary Loebner
Director, Manufacturing
& Sales Service: Lorinda Reichert
Director, Sales & Marketing: Richard A. Smeby
Editorial Director: Kenneth Winchester
Executive Editor: Bob Doyle

SUNSET PUBLISHING CORPORATION
Chairman: Jim Nelson
President/Chief Executive Officer: Robin Wolaner
Chief Financial Officer: James E. Mitchell
Publisher: Stephen J. Seabolt
Circulation Director: Robert I. Gursha
Editor, Sunset Magazine: William R. Marken
Senior Editor, Food & Entertaining: Jerry Anne Di Vecchio

All the recipes in this book were developed and tested in the
Sunset test kitchens. For information about any Sunset Book
please call 1-800-634-3095.

The nutritional data provided for each recipe is for a single
serving, based on the number of servings and the amount of each
ingredient. If a range is given for the number of servings and/or
the amount of an ingredient, the analysis is based on the average
of the figures given. The nutritional analysis does not include
optional ingredients or those for which no specific amount is
stated. If an ingredient is listed with a substitution, the data
was calculated using the first choice.

Nutritional analysis of recipes: Hill Nutrition
Associates, Inc. of Florida.

Sunset Creative Cooking Library
was produced by St. Remy Press

President: Pierre Léveillé
Managing Editor: Carolyn Jackson
Managing Art Director: Diane Denoncourt
Senior Editor: Elizabeth Cameron
Art Director: Chantal Bilodeau
Editorial Assistant: Jennifer Meltzer
Administrator: Natalie Watanabe
Production Manager: Michelle Turbide
System Coordinator: Éric Beaulieu
Proofreader: Veronica Schami
Indexer: Christine Jacobs

The following persons also assisted in the preparation
of this book: Philippe Arnoldi, Maryse Doray, Lorraine Doré,
Dominique Gagné, Geneviève Monette.

COVER: Skirt Steak with Fresh Herbs (page 25)

PHOTOGRAPHY
*Victor Budnik: 11, 56; **Robert Chartier:** 6, 7, 9, 10;*
*Peter Christiansen: Inside cover, 20, 50; **Norman A. Plate:***
*12, 46; **Kevin Sanchez:** 28; **Darrow M. Watt:** 4, 30, 60;*
*Weber-Stephen Products Co.: 5, 7, 9;.**Tom Wyatt:** Cover,*
*3, 16, 22, 26, 34, 42, 62;.**Nikolay Zurek:** 36, 52.*

ILLUSTRATION
Sally Shimizu: 8.

Special thanks to Weber-Stephen Products Co., Palatine, Ill.

Table of Contents

Barbecuing Basics

Whether you're an occasional backyard chef or a confirmed barbecue cook, you'll find recipe ideas in this book for informal picnics, family meals, and elegant dinners.

There are three main types of barbecues —charcoal-fired, gas, and electric—as shown on the opposite page. Your choice will depend on where you'll use your barbecue, the number of people you'll usually be serving, and the kinds of food you're most likely to barbecue.

Charcoal-fired barbecues. The most popular models are open braziers, covered kettles, and boxes with hinged lids.

Open braziers vary from tabletop portables and hibachis to larger models. Many have a cooking grill that can be raised or lowered to adjust the distance between the charcoal and food.

Covered kettles have dampers on the lid and under the firebox to adjust the flow of air and control the heat. They may be used, uncovered or covered, for grilling over direct heat (page 8). Kettle barbecues are available in various sizes; the 18- to 24-inch-diameter models are the most popular.

Boxes with hinged lids are similar to covered kettles, and can be used covered for cooking by indirect heat, or open or closed for grilling over direct heat.

Gas and electric barbecues. Outdoor units fueled by bottled gas usually roll on wheels; natural gas units are mounted on a fixed pedestal and are connected to a permanent gas line. Electric units are portable; they are plugged into the nearest outlet. All gas units and some electric models use a briquet-shaped material, such as lava rock, above the burner. When meat juices drip on these hot "briquets," smoke rises to penetrate and flavor the food.

Types of Barbecues

Gas barbecue

Charcoal-fired kettle

Portable charcoal-fired kettle

Electric barbecue

Portable gas barbecue

Charcoal, Starters & Fragrant Woods

Charcoal refers to the 2-inch pressed briquets, which may differ somewhat in density and composition. For best results, choose long-burning briquets, and ignite them using one of the following techniques.

Fire chimney. Stack briquets inside the chimney on top of wadded sheets of newspaper, then light. In about 30 minutes, you'll have burning coals ready to use; lift off the chimney and spread the hot coals.

Electric starter. This is one of the easiest and cleanest charcoal starters you can buy. Set the starter on a few briquets and pile more briquets on top; then plug in the starter. After 10 minutes, remove the starter from the pile; in about 20 more minutes, the coals will be ready.

Solid starter. These small, compressed, blocks or sticks light easily with a match and continue to burn until the coals are ready for cooking (about 30 minutes).

Propane starter. Simply stack the briquets around the burner; then light the burner and proceed as directed by the manufacturer.

Flavoring foods with the smoke of fragrant woods is an ancient cooking art still in style with modern patio chefs. Several popular fragrant woods are shown below.

Hickory chips

Charcoal

Mesquite chips

Basil wood chips

Barbecuing Tips

When preparing the recipes in this book, keep these tips in mind.

• The recipes were tested with the cooking grill 4 to 6 inches above the coals. If your grill is closer, the cooking time will be shorter.

• Use long-handled cooking tools to avoid burning yourself.

• Wear barbecue mitts for emergency adjustment of the grill and removal of drip pans from the fire bed.

• Use a water-filled spray bottle to extinguish flare-ups.

• Always turn food with long-handled tongs or a spatula—a long fork pierces food and allows juices to escape.

• Salt food *after* cooking (salt draws out juices).

• If using fragrant woods in a gas barbecue, the wood chips usually need to be contained in a pan and used according to the barbecue manufacturer's directions.

• Use small-mesh grills and baskets to keep small pieces of food, such as fish and vegetables from falling through the barbecue grill.

• Be sure that ashes are completely cold (sparks linger for many hours) before you dump ashes into a paper or plastic container.

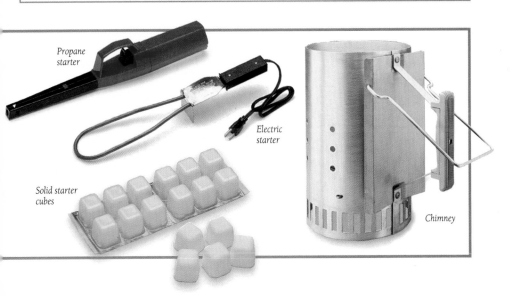

Propane starter

Electric starter

Solid starter cubes

Chimney

Two Ways to Barbecue

Direct- or indirect-heat cooking techniques differ in how the coals are arranged and in whether the barbecue is covered. For direct-heat grilling, any barbecue is satisfactory; to cook by indirect heat, you'll need a model with a lid.

By direct heat. Open the bottom dampers if your barbecue has them; for a covered barbecue, remove or open lid. Spread briquets on the fire grate in a solid layer that's 1 to 2 inches bigger all around than the grill area required for the food. Then mound the charcoal and ignite it. When the coals reach

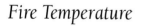

Direct heat   Indirect heat

the fire temperature specified in the recipe, spread them out into a single layer again. Set the grill at the recommended height above coals. Grease the grill, then arrange the food on the grill. To maintain an even heat, scatter 10 new briquets over the fire bed every 30 minutes.

By indirect heat. Open or remove the lid from a covered barbecue, then open the bottom dampers. Pile about 50 long-burning briquets on the fire grate and ignite them. Let the briquets burn until hot; this usually takes about 30 minutes. Using long-handled tongs, bank about half the briquets on each side of the fire grate; then place a metal drip pan in the center. Set the cooking grill 4 to 6 inches above the drip pan; lightly grease the grill. Set the food on the grill directly above the drip pan. Add 5 or 6 briquets to each side of the fire grate at 30- to 40-minute intervals to keep temperature constant.

Fire Temperature

Use the fire temperature recommended in the recipe.

Hot. You can hold your hand close to the grill for only 2 to 3 seconds. Coals are barely covered with gray ash.

Medium. You can hold your hand at grill level for 4 to 5 seconds. Coals glow red through a layer of gray ash.

Low. You can hold your hand at grill level for at least 6 to 7 seconds. Coals are covered with a thick layer of ash.

Barbecue Accessories

This array of barbecue accessories contains some of the equipment that outdoor chefs should have on hand. Protect your clothing by wearing an apron. A metal brush cleans the grill if it is still hot. The mitt and long-handled tools protect your hands.

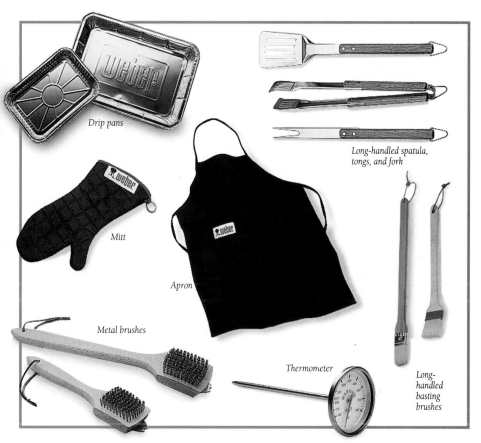

Drip pans

Long-handled spatula, tongs, and fork

Mitt

Apron

Metal brushes

Thermometer

Long-handled basting brushes

Skewer Savvy

Skewers make some foods easier to handle on the grill by:

• Controlling small bits of food. Threaded onto skewers, the pieces become a single unit to lift and turn.

• Keeping foods flat. Whole birds that have been split and pressed open have less tendency to pull back when a skewer is threaded through the bird from shoulder to shoulder. Heavy parallel skewers threaded through a boneless leg of lamb makes it easier to manage; insert skewers so that they cross near the tips.

When loading skewers, keep in mind that meat, poultry, firm-texture fish, and shellfish shrink as they cook, tightening their hold on the skewer. Most everything else gets softer or more fragile.

Vegetables and fruit, in particular, tend to soften as they cook and lose their grip. Parallel skewers in these foods give them support and keep them from spinning or flopping. You get maximum control by pushing two skewers perpendicularly through foods, each about ⅓ of the distance in from opposite ends of the food.

Crisp or firm vegetables and fruit tend to split when pushed onto thick skewers; slender, sharply pointed metal or bamboo skewers work best for these foods. To keep bamboo skewers from charring while they're on the grill, soak the skewers for 30 minutes in water before using.

Foods that fall apart when cooked (such as sole or other flaky fish) are not suitable for skewering.

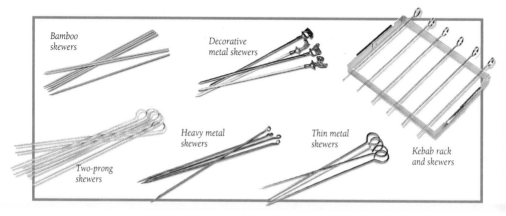

Bamboo skewers

Decorative metal skewers

Two-prong skewers

Heavy metal skewers

Thin metal skewers

Kebab rack and skewers

Grilling Fruits

Before grilling, prepare fruits as directed below. If using small pieces of fruit, thread on thin metal or bamboo skewers ahead of time, making sure fruit lies flat. Coat prepared fruits with plain or seasoned butter or basting sauce used on an accompanying entrée, then place fruit on a lightly greased grill 4 to 6 inches above a lightly dispersed bed of medium coals. Cook, turning frequently, until hot and streaked with brown.

Apples

Core apples, peel, if desired. Cut small apples into halves; cut larger apples crosswise into ¼-inch-thick rings.
Grilling time: About 6 minutes for rings; 10 to 12 minutes for halves.

Apricots

Cut into halves; discard pits; thread on skewers, making sure fruit lies flat.
Grilling time: 4 to 6 minutes.

Bananas

Do not peel. Cut into halves lengthwise.
Grilling time: 4 to 6 minutes.

Figs

Cut into halves lengthwise; thread on skewers, making sure fruit lies flat.
Grilling time: 4 to 6 minutes.

Nectarines

Cut into halves lengthwise; discard pits.
Grilling time: 6 to 8 minutes.

Oranges or tangerines

Do not peel. Cut small oranges into halves crosswise; cut large ones crosswise into ¾-inch-thick slices.
Grilling time: 4 to 5 minutes for slices; 10 to 12 minutes for halves.

Papayas

Peel, if desired; then cut crosswise into ¾-inch-thick rings or cut lengthwise into quarters. Remove and discard seeds.
Grilling time: 5 to 8 minutes.

Peaches

Peel and cut into halves lengthwise; discard pits.
Grilling time: 6 to 8 minutes.

Pears

Peel, if desired. Cut small pears into halves lengthwise; cut large pears into ¼-inch-wide wedges; remove cores; thread on skewers, making sure fruit lies flat.
Grilling time: About 6 minutes for wedges; 10 to 12 minutes for halves.

LAMB

A touch of added flavor is all you need to enhance the distinctive taste of barbecued lamb with its subtle hint of the wild. Many of the recipes in the pages that follow contain marinades and bastes of fruits or herbs to complement the meat.

GREEK SHISH KEBAB, RECIPE ON PAGE 14

Greek Shish Kebab

(PICTURED ON PAGE 12)

Marinated lamb and vegetables combine in this traditional favorite.

◆

PER SERVING: *374 calories, 34 g protein, 12 mg carbohydrates, 21 g total fat, 101 mg cholesterol, 87 mg sodium*

PREPARATION TIME: *20 min.*
MARINATING TIME: *4 hr.*
GRILLING TIME: *15 min.*

⅓ cup olive oil or salad oil
3 Tbsp. lemon juice
1 large onion, finely
   chopped
2 bay leaves
2 tsp. oregano leaves
½ tsp. black pepper
2 lb. lean boneless lamb
   (leg or shoulder), cut
   into 1½-inch cubes
1 large mild red onion,
   cut into 1-inch pieces
1 large green or red bell
   pepper, seeded, cut
   into 1½-inch squares
½ lb. medium-size
   mushrooms
About 1 cup cherry
   tomatoes

In a large nonreactive bowl, stir together oil, lemon juice, chopped onion, bay leaves, oregano, and black pepper. Reserve ¼ cup of marinade. Add lamb; stir to coat. Cover and refrigerate for at least 4 hours or until next day, stirring several times.

Lift meat from marinade and drain briefly (discard marinade). To reserved marinade, add red onion, bell pepper, and mushrooms; turn to coat, then lift out. On 6 sturdy metal skewers, thread meat alternately with vegetables.

Place skewers on a lightly greased grill 4 to 6 inches above a solid bed of medium coals. Cook, turning and basting frequently with reserved marinade until meat and vegetables are well browned but meat is still pink in center (10 to 15 minutes); cut to test. Garnish with tomatoes.

Makes 6 servings

Blackberry Shish Kebab

Blackberry syrup gives kebabs of lamb and water chestnuts a fruity sweetness.

◆

PER SERVING: *285 calories, 30 g protein, 22 g carbohydrates, 8 g total fat, 91 g cholesterol, 283 mg sodium*

PREPARATION TIME: *45 min.*
MARINATING TIME: *4 hr.*
GRILLING TIME: *8 min.*

½ *cup blackberry syrup*
¼ *cup red wine vinegar*
2 *Tbsp. each soy sauce*
 and chopped fresh mint
2 *cloves garlic, minced*
 or pressed
½ *tsp. pepper*
2 *cans (about 8 oz. each)*
 whole water chestnuts,
 drained
1½ *lb. lean boneless lamb*
 (leg or shoulder), cut
 into 1-inch cubes

In a nonreactive bowl, stir together syrup, vinegar, soy, mint, garlic, and pepper. Add water chestnuts and lamb to marinade; stir to coat. Cover and refrigerate for at least 4 hours, stirring several times.

Lift meat and water chestnuts from marinade and drain briefly (discard marinade). Thread meat and water chestnuts alternately on thin bamboo (see page 10) or metal skewers. To avoid splitting water chestnuts, rotate skewer as you pierce them.

Place skewers on a lightly greased grill 4 to 6 inches above a solid bed of medium coals. Cook, turning occasionally, until meat is well browned on outside but still pink in center (about 8 minutes); cut to test.

Makes 4 or 5 servings

Shish Kebab with Apricots

These brightly colored kebabs are flavored with a fresh-tasting orange juice marinade.

◆

PER SERVING: *431 calories, 38 g protein, 16 g carbohydrates, 24 g total fat, 114 mg cholesterol, 348 mg sodium*

PREPARATION TIME: *1 hr.*
MARINATING TIME: *4 hr.*
GRILLING TIME: *15 min.*

1 tsp. grated orange zest
⅔ cup orange juice
½ cup olive oil or salad oil
3 Tbsp. white wine vinegar
2 Tbsp. soy sauce
1¼ tsp. dry rosemary
½ cup minced shallots
2 cloves garlic, minced
   or pressed
⅛ tsp. pepper
3 lb. lean boneless lamb
   (leg or shoulder), cut into
   1½-inch cubes
24 to 30 dried apricots
1 large onion, cut into
   1½-inch squares
3 medium-size red bell
   peppers, seeded, cut into
   1½-inch squares

In a large nonreactive bowl, combine orange zest, orange juice, oil, white wine vinegar, soy sauce, rosemary, shallots, garlic, and pepper; reserve ½ cup of marinade. Add lamb and apricots to remaining marinade; stir to coat. Cover and refrigerate for at least 4 hours or until next day, stirring several times.

Lift meat and apricots from sauce and drain briefly (discard marinade). On 8 sturdy metal skewers, thread meat alternately with apricots, onion, and bell pepper.

Place skewers on a lightly greased grill 4 to 6 inches above a solid bed of medium coals. Cook, turning occasionally and basting frequently with reserved sauce, until meat is well browned on outside but still pink in center (about 12 to 15 minutes); cut to test.

Makes 8 servings

Lamb Sosaties

A chile-sparked curry marinade sets off the robust flavor of the lamb.

◆

PER SERVING: *308 calories, 39 g protein, 12 g carbohydrates, 11 g total fat, 121 mg cholesterol, 98 mg sodium*

PREPARATION TIME: *30 min.*
MARINATING TIME: *4 hr.*
GRILLING TIME: *15 min.*

4 lb. lean boneless lamb
(leg or shoulder), cut
into 1½-inch cubes
1½ cups cider vinegar
3 Tbsp. apricot or pineapple
jam
1½ Tbsp. each curry powder
and firmly packed
brown sugar
4 small dried hot red chiles,
crushed
2 medium-size onions,
thinly sliced
3 cloves garlic, minced
or pressed
2 bay leaves

Place lamb in a large bowl; set aside. In a small pan, stir together vinegar, jam, curry powder, sugar, chiles, onions, garlic, and bay leaves. Bring to a boil over high heat, then remove from heat and let cool. Pour vinegar mixture through a strainer; discard residue in strainer. Reserve ½ cup. Pour remaining marinade over meat in bowl; stir meat to coat. Cover and refrigerate for at least 4 hours, stirring several times.

Lift meat from marinade and drain briefly (discard marinade). Thread meat equally on about 10 sturdy metal skewers. Place skewers on a lightly greased grill 4 to 6 inches above a solid bed of medium coals. Cook, turning often and basting with reserved marinade, until meat is well browned on outside but still pink in center (12 to 15 minutes); cut to test.

Makes 10 servings

Shaslik

Lamb cubes are seasoned with a wine marinade.

◆

PER SERVING: *216 calories, 25 g protein, 8 g carbohydrates, 8 g total fat, 76 mg cholesterol, 72 mg sodium*

PREPARATION TIME: *35 min.*
MARINATING TIME: *2 hr.*
GRILLING TIME: *8 to 10 min.*

1 small onion, finely
  chopped
1 Tbsp. each *salad oil*
  and Worcestershire
1 bay leaf
1 clove garlic, minced
  or pressed
¼ tsp. pepper
2 Tbsp. chopped parsley
1 tsp. dry oregano
1 cup dry red wine
2 lb. boneless leg of lamb,
  trimmed of fat
1 lb. small onions, each
about 1 inch in diameter
2 medium-size red bell
  peppers, seeded, cut into
  1-inch squares
Salt and pepper

In a nonreactive bowl, mix together chopped onion, oil, Worcestershire, bay leaf, garlic, pepper, parsley, oregano, and wine; reserve ¼ cup of marinade.

Cut lamb into 1-inch cubes; place in a heavy plastic bag set in a bowl. To bag, add remaining marinade. Seal bag and turn to mix ingredients. Refrigerate for at least 2 hours.

Meanwhile, in a 3-quart pan, combine small whole onions with water to cover. Bring to a boil; reduce heat and boil gently for 5 minutes. Drain and peel onions.

Remove lamb from bag (discard marinade). Thread onto 8 long metal skewers, alternating lamb with small whole onions and red pepper squares. Place skewers on a lightly greased grill 4 to 6 inches above a solid bed of hot coals. Cook, brushing with reserved marinade and turning as needed, until lamb is evenly browned but still pink in center; cut to test (8 to 10 minutes total). Season to taste with salt and pepper.

Makes 8 servings

Shish Kebabs with Sumac

Do not confuse this fragrant spice with the poisonous sumacs of North America.

◆

PER SERVING: *243 calories, 34 g protein, 3 g carbohydrates, 9 g total fat, 103 mg cholesterol, 104 mg sodium*

PREPARATION TIME: *20 min.*
MARINATING TIME: *30 min.*
GRILLING TIME: *10 min.*

About ⅓ cup ground sumac
2 tsp. minced fresh ginger
½ tsp. ground allspice
½ tsp. crushed dried hot red chiles
2 lb. boned and fat-trimmed lamb leg, cut in 1-inch cubes
2 cloves garlic, minced or pressed
About 1 cup plain low-fat yogurt
Salt and pepper

In a bowl, mix together sumac, ginger, allspice, and chiles. Add lamb and garlic; mix well. Cover and refrigerate for at least 30 minutes, stirring several times. Lift meat from marinade and drain briefly (discard marinade). Thread meat onto sturdy metal skewers, keeping the pieces slightly apart.

Place skewers on a lightly greased grill 4 to 6 inches above a solid bed of medium coals. Cook, turning frequently, until meat is well browned on outside but still pink in center (about 10 minutes); cut to test. Serve with yogurt and additional sumac. Add salt and pepper to taste.

Makes 6 servings

BEEF & PORK

*R*obust kebabs of barbecued beef, flavored with assertive marinades and sauces, are easy to prepare, yet sure to please. In this section of the book, you'll also find recipes that bring together the rich flavor of pork with crisp bell peppers, corn, and apples.

INDONESIAN BEEF SKEWERS, RECIPE ON PAGE 24

Indonesian Beef Skewers

(PICTURED ON PAGE 22)

Satay is probably the best-known Southeast Asian meat dish.

◆

PER SERVING: *286 g calories, 29 g protein, 2 g carbohydrates, 17 g total fat, 92 mg cholesterol, 684 mg sodium*

PREPARATION TIME: *45 min.*
MARINATING TIME: *2 hr.*
GRILLING TIME: *10 min.*

3 *cloves garlic, minced
    or pressed*
5 *Tbsp. soy sauce*
1 *Tbsp. salad oil*
1¼ *tsp. each ground cumin
    and ground coriander*
1½ *lb. boneless top sirloin
    steak, cut into 1-inch cubes*
4½ *Tbsp. lemon juice*
1 *cup water*
⅔ *cup creamy peanut butter*
2 *Tbsp. firmly packed
    brown sugar*
¼ to ½ *tsp. crushed red
    pepper flakes*

In a bowl, combine 1 clove garlic, 2 tablespoons soy sauce, oil, and 1 teaspoon each of cumin and coriander. Add meat and stir to coat; cover and refrigerate for at least 2 hours, stirring occasionally.

In a nonreactive bowl, mix 3 tablespoons lemon juice, 2 tablespoons soy sauce, remaining cumin and coriander to make a basting sauce.

In a 2-quart pan, combine water, peanut butter, and 2 cloves garlic. Cook over medium-low heat, stirring, until mixture boils and thickens. Remove from heat and stir in brown sugar, remaining lemon juice and soy sauce, and crushed red pepper.

Lift meat from marinade and drain briefly (discard marinade). Thread 4 or 5 pieces of meat on each skewer. Arrange skewers on a lightly greased grill 2 to 4 inches above a solid bed of hot coals. Cook, turning often, until well browned (about 8 to 10 minutes for medium-rare); cut to test. About 3 minutes before meat is done, brush with basting sauce. Stir peanut sauce over low heat and serve with skewers.

Makes 4 to 6 servings

Skirt Steaks with Fresh Herbs

Fresh herbs add a tantalizing quality to barbecued beef.

◆

PER SERVING: *394 g calories, 26 g protein, 3 g carbohydrates, 31 g total fat, 66 mg cholesterol, 156 mg sodium*

PREPARATION TIME: *30 min.*
MARINATING TIME: *4 hr.*
GRILLING TIME: *6 min.*

*1½ lb. skirt steak, trimmed
of excess fat*
½ cup olive oil
3 Tbsp. red wine vinegar
1 Tbsp. Dijon mustard
*1 clove garlic, minced
or pressed*
¼ tsp. pepper
*25 to 30 fresh thyme,
rosemary, or tarragon
sprigs, each about 3
inches long*

Cut steak crosswise into about 12-inch lengths, then arrange in a 9- by 13-inch dish. In a small nonreactive bowl, mix oil, vinegar, mustard, garlic, and pepper; reserve ¼ cup of marinade. Pour remaining marinade over meat; turn meat to coat. Cover and refrigerate for at least 4 hours or until next day, turning occasionally.

Soak herb sprigs in water to cover for about 30 minutes.

Lift meat from marinade and drain briefly (discard marinade). Weave each piece of meat onto a long metal skewer, rippling meat very slightly and tucking an herb sprig between skewer and meat on both sides of meat.

Place skewers on a lightly greased grill 4 to 6 inches above a solid bed of hot coals. Cook, turning often and basting with reserved marinade, until done (5 to 6 minutes for rare); cut to test.

Makes 6 servings

Skewered Beef & Corn

Pineapple juice and red wine flavor these economical kebabs.

◆

PER SERVING: 690 calories, 56 g protein, 34 g carbohydrates, 36 g total fat, 196 mg cholesterol, 200 mg sodium

PREPARATION TIME: *30 min.*
MARINATING TIME: *6 hr.*
GRILLING TIME: *15 min.*

4-lb. boneless chuck roast,
 tenderized
1½ cups each canned
 pineapple juice and
 red wine
1½ Tbsp. instant minced
 onion
1½ tsp. each Worcestershire
 and thyme
¾ tsp. dry mustard
¼ cup firmly packed
 brown sugar
¼ tsp. pepper
2 cloves garlic, minced
 or pressed
¼ cup melted butter
¼ cup salad oil
5 ears corn, husked
3 green bell peppers, seeded
2 mild red onions
1 pineapple, peeled, cored

Cut meat into 1½-inch cubes and place in a large bowl. In a nonreactive bowl, stir together pineapple juice, wine, onion, Worcestershire, thyme, mustard, sugar, pepper, and garlic; reserve ⅓ cup. Pour remaining marinade over meat; stir to coat. Cover and refrigerate for at least 6 hours, stirring occasionally. Lift meat from bowl and drain briefly (discard marinade).

In a bowl, stir together butter, oil, and reserved marinade; set aside. Cut corn into 2-inch lengths; cut peppers and onions into 1½-inch pieces; cut pineapple into 1½-inch cubes. On long, sturdy metal skewers, thread meat alternately with corn, bell peppers, onions, and pineapple. Brush with butter mixture. Place skewers on a lightly greased grill 4 to 6 inches above a solid bed of hot coals. Cook, turning and basting with butter mixture, until meat is done (15 minutes for medium-rare); cut to test.

Makes 8 servings

Grilled Beef & Peppers

Here's an appealingly colorful meat-and-vegetable combination.

◆

PER SERVING: *196 calories, 28 g protein, 6 g carbohydrates, 6 g total fat, 72 mg cholesterol, 56 mg sodium*

PREPARATION TIME: *20 min.*
MARINATING TIME: *30 min.*
GRILLING TIME: *8 min.*

1 *Tbsp. lemon juice*
1 *tsp. olive oil*
⅓ *cup dry red wine*
1½ *lb. boneless beef top
    round (about ½ inch
    thick), trimmed of fat*
1 *each small green, red,
    and yellow bell pepper,
    cut lengthwise into
    sixths, seeded*
12 *rosemary sprigs (each
    about 3 inches long)*
Salt and pepper

Set a large heavy-duty plastic bag in a shallow pan. In bag, combine lemon juice, oil, and wine; reserve 4 tablespoons of marinade.

Cut beef across the grain into 6 strips; place between sheets of plastic wrap; pound with flat side of a meat mallet until each piece is about ¼ inch thick. Add beef strips and peppers to bag; seal bag and turn to coat beef and peppers with marinade. Refrigerate for at least 30 minutes.

Lift beef and peppers from bag and drain briefly (discard marinade). On each of 6 long metal skewers, weave one beef strip and 3 bell pepper pieces (one of each color), rippling beef slightly around peppers. For each skewer, tuck 2 rosemary sprigs between meat and skewer.

Place skewers on a lightly greased grill 4 to 6 inches above a solid bed of hot coals. Cook, turning and brushing with reserved marinade, until meat is done (6 to 8 minutes for rare); cut to test. Season with salt and pepper.

Makes 6 servings

Red Bell Pepper
& Sausage Loaf

Here's a party-size sandwich that's easy to put together.

◆

PER SERVING: *611 calories, 28 g protein, 43 g carbohydrates, 36 g total fat, 102 mg cholesterol, 1,349 mg sodium*

PREPARATION TIME: *15 min.*
GRILLING TIME: *8 min.*

6 *mild Italian sausages
(1¼ to 1½ lb. total)*
¼ *cup butter or margarine*
1 *clove garlic, minced
or pressed*
1 *long loaf (1 lb.) French
bread, cut in half
horizontally*
2 *large red bell peppers,
seeded, cut lengthwise
into 1½-inch-wide strips*
6 *oz. sliced mozzarella
or provolone cheese*
Prepared mustard

Prick sausages in several places, then place in a wide frying pan and add water to cover. Bring to a boil over high heat; reduce heat to low, cover, and simmer for 5 minutes. Drain sausages and set aside.

Melt butter in a small pan over medium heat; stir in garlic. Brush garlic butter evenly over cut side of each bread half; set aside.

On a metal skewer at least 12 inches long, thread sausages and bell pepper strips, running skewer through center of each sausage and pepper strip.

Place on a lightly greased grill 4 to 6 inches above a solid bed of hot coals. Cook, turning occasionally, until sausages are well browned on outside and hot throughout (5 to 8 minutes). Set bread halves, cut side down, on grill. Cook just until bread is streaked with brown (1 to 2 minutes).

Overlap cheese slices on one bread half. Top with sausage-pepper skewer; set top of bread in place, and pull out skewer. Cut into 6 portions; add mustard to taste.

Makes 6 servings

Chinese Pork Appetizers

These savory morsels hot from the grill make a great start to a meal.

◆

PER SERVING: *69 calories, 8 g protein, .34 g carbohydrates, 4 g total fat, 22 mg cholesterol, 149 mg sodium*

PREPARATION TIME: *10 min.*
MARINATING TIME: *2 hr.*
GRILLING TIME: *10 min.*

¼ cup soy sauce
2 Tbsp. salad oil
2 cloves garlic, minced or pressed
1 small dried hot red chile, crushed
½ tsp. sugar
¼ tsp. anise seeds
⅛ tsp. each cinnamon and cloves
2 lb. lean boneless pork

In a bowl, combine soy sauce, oil, garlic, chile, sugar, anise seeds, cinnamon, and cloves. Cut pork into ¼- to ½-inch-thick strips about 1 inch wide. Stir into soy mixture; cover and refrigerate for 1 to 2 hours, stirring several times.

Lift pork from marinade and drain briefly (discard marinade). Thread meat onto small metal skewers, using 1 or 2 strips per skewer. Place on a lightly greased grill 4 to 6 inches above a solid bed of medium coals. Cook, turning occasionally, until browned on outside but no longer pink in center (7 to 10 minutes); cut to test.

Makes 2 dozen appetizers

Pork Satay Balinese

The mouth-watering succulence of barbecued pork is hard to resist.

◆

PER SERVING: *246 calories, 25 g protein, 14 g carbohydrates, 10 g total fat, 77 mg cholesterol, 315 mg sodium*

PREPARATION TIME: *15 min.*
MARINATING TIME: *2 hr.*
GRILLING TIME: *15 min.*

2 *lb. boneless fresh leg*
of pork or pork loin,
trimmed of fat
½ *cup Major Grey's*
chutney
¼ *cup catsup*
1 *Tbsp. each salad oil*
and soy sauce
4 *drops liquid hot pepper*
seasoning
¼ *cup very finely chopped*
dry-roast peanuts
Cilantro sprigs

Cut pork into 1-inch cubes. In a blender or food processor, combine chutney, catsup, oil, soy sauce, and hot pepper seasoning; whirl until smooth. Reserve ¼ cup of marinade. Place pork cubes in a heavy plastic bag set in a shallow pan. Add remaining marinade and seal bag, turning to coat. Refrigerate for at least 2 hours or until next day.

Lift pork from bag and drain briefly (discard marinade). Thread onto 8 skewers. Arrange on a lightly greased grill 4 to 6 inches above a solid bed of medium-hot coals. Cook, basting once or twice with reserved marinade, turning as needed, until browned on all sides (12 to 15 minutes). Arrange on a serving dish, sprinkle with peanuts, and garnish with cilantro.

Makes 8 servings

Miso-marinated Pork
with Apple & Onion

Aka miso, a red fermented soybean paste, is available in Asian markets.

◆

PER SERVING: *177 calories, 15 g protein, 21 g carbohydrates, 4 g total fat, 40 mg cholesterol, 444 mg sodium*

PREPARATION TIME: *25 min.*
MARINATING TIME: *1 hr.*
GRILLING TIME: *10 min.*

1 *lb. pork tenderloin, trimmed of fat*
⅓ *cup each aka miso and maple syrup*
¼ *cup sake, dry white wine, or water*
2 *Tbsp. minced fresh ginger*
2 *medium-size apples such as McIntosh or Fuji*
Lemon juice
1 *large onion, cut into wedges, layers separated*

Cut pork into ⅛-inch-thick, 6- to 7-inch-long slices. In a heavy plastic bag set in a shallow pan, combine miso, syrup, sake, and ginger; reserve ¼ cup of marinade. Add pork and seal bag, turning to coat. Refrigerate for at least 1 hour.

Core apples, cut into ½-inch wedges, and brush with lemon juice to prevent darkening. Lift pork slices from bag and drain briefly (discard marinade).

To assemble each skewer, thread tip of a thin metal skewer through end of a pork slice; thread on a piece of onion and an apple wedge, then thread skewer through pork again. Repeat process until skewer is full; you should have 8 skewers total.

Place skewers on a grill 4 to 6 inches above a solid bed of medium coals. Cook, basting with reserved marinade and turning often, until meat is no longer pink in center (about 10 minutes); cut to test.

Makes 8 servings

CHICKEN & TURKEY

*C*hicken cooked over glowing coals takes on a gloriously rich golden color, yet it remains succulent and tasty. Even better, it's easy to flavor the meat in pleasing ways, with marinades, sauces, and simple butter bastes.

CURRIED CHICKEN & FRUIT KEBABS, RECIPE ON PAGE 38

Curried Chicken & Fruit Kebabs

(PICTURED ON PAGE 36)

Skewer tropical fruits with chunks of chicken breast for a great appetizer.

◆

PER SERVING: 137 calories, 11 g protein, 13 g carbohydrates, 5 g total fat, 26 mg cholesterol, 162 mg sodium

PREPARATION TIME: *25 min.*
MARINATING TIME: *2 hr.*
GRILLING TIME: *12 min.*

3 *whole chicken breasts*
   (about 3 lb. total), split,
   skinned, boned
¾ *cup bottled oil and*
   vinegar salad dressing
2 *tsp. curry powder*
3 *medium-size green-tipped*
   bananas
1 *medium-size papaya or*
   20 preserved kumquats,
   drained
2 *cups fresh pineapple*
   chunks
⅓ *cup honey*
Lime wedges

Cut chicken into bite-size pieces (you should have at least 60). Mix salad dressing and curry powder; reserve ¼ cup marinade. Add chicken to remaining marinade, stirring gently to coat. Cover and refrigerate for at least 2 hours or until next day.

Shortly before cooking, peel bananas and cut into 1-inch slices; brush with reserved marinade. Peel, halve, and seed papaya; cut into 1-inch cubes. Lift chicken from marinade and drain briefly (discard marinade). Alternately thread chicken on bamboo skewers (see page 10) with 1 piece each pineapple, banana, and papaya. Stir honey into remaining reserved marinade and brush over kebabs.

Place skewers on a lightly greased grill 4 to 6 inches above a solid bed of hot coals. Cook, turning once and brushing with marinade, until chicken is no longer pink in center (about 12 minutes); cut to test. Serve with lime.

Makes 20 appetizers

Fig & Chicken Skewers

Ripe figs and dark-meat chicken are perfect for grilling on a hibachi.

◆

PER SERVING: *233 calories, 21 g protein, 25 g carbohydrates, 4 g total fat, 81 mg cholesterol, 623 mg sodium*

PREPARATION TIME: *20 min.*
MARINATING TIME: *30 min.*
GRILLING TIME: *8 min.*

½ cup sake or dry sherry
¼ cup each soy sauce
and sugar
5 *chicken thighs (about*
1½ lb. total), skinned,
boned, each cut into
4 equal pieces
5 *large ripe figs, stems*
trimmed, cut lengthwise
into quarters
4 *green onions, root ends*
trimmed, cut into 1½-
inch lengths
Lemon wedges

In a 1- to 1½-quart pan, combine sake, soy sauce, and sugar. Bring to a boil, stirring until sugar is dissolved. Remove from heat, pour into a large bowl and let cool to room temperature. Reserve ¼ cup of sauce.

Rinse chicken and pat dry. Add figs, onions, and chicken to sauce in bowl; mix gently to coat evenly. Cover and refrigerate for 30 minutes.

Drain sauce into a 1- to 1½-quart pan; bring to a boil. Pour through a fine wire strainer, and set aside.

Thread 1 piece of chicken, 1 fig piece, and 3 or 4 green onion pieces on one end of each of 20 bamboo (see page 10) or metal skewers. Place skewers on a lightly greased grill 2 inches above a solid bed of hot coals. Cook, turning and basting with reserved sauce, until chicken is no longer pink in center (6 to 8 minutes); cut to test.

Serve with remaining reserved sauce and lemon.

Makes 4 servings

Fajita Chicken Skewers

Fajitas come off the grill faster if you start with marinated meat.

◆

PER SERVING: 532 calories, 33 g protein, 52 g carbohydrates, 21 g total fat, 66 mg cholesterol, 439 sodium

PREPARATION TIME: *15 min.*
MARINATING TIME: *1 hr.*
GRILLING TIME: *10 min.*

½ each *lime juice and salad oil*
¼ cup each *beer and firmly packed brown sugar*
1 large *onion, thinly sliced*
1 clove *garlic, minced or pressed*
2 fresh *jalapeño chiles, seeded, minced*
2 Tbsp. each *ground cumin and paprika*
1 Tbsp. *Worcestershire*
1 tsp. *pepper*
1 lb. *skinless, boneless chicken breasts, cut into ¾-inch cubes*
8 *flour tortillas (each about 8 inches in diameter)*
Shredded Cheddar cheese, guacamole, and sour cream (optional)

In a large nonreactive bowl, combine lime juice, oil, beer, sugar, onion, garlic, chiles, cumin, paprika, Worcestershire, and pepper. Add chicken and stir to coat; cover and refrigerate for at least 1 hour or up to 8 hours.

Lift chicken from marinade and drain briefly (discard marinade). Thread chicken equally on 4 metal skewers. Sprinkle each tortilla with a few drops of water; then stack tortillas and wrap in heavy-duty foil.

Place chicken on a lightly greased grill 4 to 6 inches above a solid bed of hot coals. Place tortillas at edge of grill (not above coals). Cook, turning chicken and tortillas occasionally, until tortillas are warm and chicken is lightly browned on outside and no longer pink in center (about 10 minutes); cut to test.

To eat, place chicken on a tortilla; top with cheese, guacamole, and sour cream, if desired. Roll to enclose, then eat out of hand.

Makes 4 servings

Grilled Turkey Chunks Piccata

For simple summer fare, try tender, caper-topped turkey chunks.

◆

PER SERVING: *228 calories, 39 g protein, 5 g carbohydrates, 6 g total fat, 94 mg cholesterol, 192 mg sodium*

PREPARATION TIME: *15 min.*
MARINATING TIME: *30 min.*
GRILLING TIME: *15 min.*

3 Tbsp. capers with liquid
½ cup lemon juice
2 Tbsp. olive oil
¼ tsp. pepper
2 lb. skinless, boneless
   turkey breast, cut into
   1-inch cubes
4 medium-size zucchini
Lemon wedges

Drain caper liquid into a shallow nonreactive dish; cover drained capers and refrigerate. Stir lemon juice, oil, and pepper into caper liquid; reserve ¼ cup. Add turkey to remaining marinade and stir to coat. Cover and refrigerate for at least 30 minutes or up to 2 hours.

Lift turkey from marinade and drain briefly (discard marinade). Thread turkey equally on 6 metal skewers. Cut each zucchini in half lengthwise; coat zucchini with reserved marinade.

Place turkey and zucchini on a lightly greased grill 4 to 6 inches above a solid bed of medium coals. Cook, turning as needed and basting several times with reserved marinade, until turkey is no longer pink in center (about 15 minutes); cut to test. Sprinkle with drained capers; offer lemon wedges to squeeze over meat.

Makes 6 servings

Chicken Kebabs Shanghai

Skewers of chicken and fresh pineapple are flavored with a ginger-orange marinade.

◆

PER SERVING: *299 calories, 33 g protein, 31 g carbohydrates, 5 g total fat, 79 mg cholesterol, 334 mg sodium*

PREPARATION TIME: *30 min.*
MARINATING TIME: *30 min.*
GRILLING TIME: *12 min.*

¾ tsp. grated orange zest
⅓ cup orange juice
3 Tbsp. firmly packed
   brown sugar
2 Tbsp. soy sauce
4 tsp. each minced fresh
   ginger and red wine
   vinegar
1 Tbsp. Oriental sesame
   oil or salad oil
½ tsp. ground coriander
1½ lb. skinned, boned
   chicken breasts, cut into
   1½-inch chunks
1 medium-size pineapple,
   peeled, cored, cut into
   1-inch chunks

In a medium-size bowl, mix orange zest, orange juice, sugar, soy sauce, ginger, vinegar, oil, and coriander; reserve ¼ cup marinade. Stir chicken in remaining marinade. Cover and refrigerate for at least 30 minutes or up to 2 hours.

Lift chicken from marinade and drain briefly (discard marinade). Thread chicken and pineapple chunks on thin metal skewers, alternating 2 chicken chunks and 1 pineapple chunk. Brush reserved marinade over pineapple. Place skewers on a lightly greased grill 4 to 6 inches above a solid bed of hot coals. Cook, turning and basting with reserved marinade, until chicken is no longer pink in center (6 to 8 minutes); cut to test.

Makes 4 to 6 servings

Chicken with Bay, Squash & Tomatoes

Bay leaves and a mustardy vinaigrette flavor chicken thighs, squash, and cherry tomatoes.

◆

PER SERVING: *565 calories, 42 g protein, 12 g carbohydrates, 39 g total fat, 146 mg cholesterol, 251 mg sodium*

PREPARATION TIME: *20 min.*
MARINATING TIME: *6 hr.*
GRILLING TIME: *40 min.*

12 chicken thighs (about
    4 lb. total), skinned, if
    desired
3 Tbsp. each Dijon mustard
    and white wine vinegar
¾ cup olive oil or salad oil
1 tsp. coarsely ground
    pepper
About 36 fresh bay leaves
    (or dry bay leaves soaked
    in hot water for 1 hour)
4 medium-size crookneck
    squash, cut into ½-inch-
    thick slices
3 cups cherry tomatoes,
    stemmed

Rinse chicken and pat dry. In a nonreactive bowl, stir together mustard, vinegar, oil, pepper, and 6 bay leaves. Add chicken and turn to coat. Cover and refrigerate for at least 6 hours, turning occasionally.

Lift chicken from marinade and drain briefly. Add squash to marinade and stir to coat; then lift out squash and bay leaves. Discard marinade.

On 3 of 9 sturdy metal skewers, each about 10 inches long, alternate chicken with 12 of the bay leaves (including those from marinade); pierce chicken perpendicular to bone. On 3 more skewers, thread squash, piercing it through skin, and about half the remaining bay leaves. Thread tomatoes and remaining bay leaves on remaining 3 skewers.

Place chicken on a lightly greased grill 4 to 6 inches above a solid bed of medium coals. Cook, turning frequently, for 10 minutes. Place squash on grill. Continue to cook, turning squash and chicken often, until meat near thighbone is no longer pink (20 to 30 minutes); cut to test. Set tomatoes on grill; cook, turning, until hot.

Makes 6 servings

Chicken & Vegetable Bundles

Strips of chicken, wrapped around carrot and zucchini slivers, are skewered for easy grilling.

◆

PER SERVING: 219 calories, 34 g protein, 4 g carbohydrates, 6 g total fat, 92 mg cholesterol, 127 mg sodium

PREPARATION TIME: *40 min.*
GRILLING TIME: *12 min.*

4 *whole chicken breasts*
   (about 1 lb. each),
   skinned, boned, split
3 *or 4 medium-size carrots,*
   cut into 3-inch-long
   julienne strips
1 *or 2 medium-size*
   zucchini, cut into 3-inch-
   long julienne strips
3 *Tbsp. each salad oil and*
   lemon juice
¼ *tsp. each salt and dry*
   rosemary
Dash of pepper

Rinse poultry and pat dry. Using a flat-surfaced mallet, pound each chicken half-breast between 2 sheets of wax paper until ¼ inch thick. Cut each half-breast in half lengthwise. For each bundle, wrap one strip of meat around 3 or 4 strips each of carrot and zucchini. Run 2 parallel metal skewers through each bundle (one through each end); thread 2 bundles on each pair of skewers.

In a nonreactive bowl, combine oil, lemon juice, salt, rosemary, and pepper. Place skewers on a lightly greased grill 4 to 6 inches above a solid bed of medium coals. Cook, turning and brushing with oil mixture, until meat is no longer pink in center (10 to 12 minutes); cut to test.

Makes 8 servings

Chicken on a Stick
with Couscous

***B**eat the heat of a summer afternoon with this quick-cooking recipe.*

◆

PER SERVING: *574 calories, 45 g protein, 66 g carbohydrates, 12 g total fat, 82 mg cholesterol, 139 mg sodium*

PREPARATION TIME: *30 min.*
MARINATING TIME: *30 min.*
GRILLING TIME: *10 min.*

⅓ *cup each lemon juice*
  and olive oil
¼ *cup dry white wine*
7 *cloves garlic, minced*
  or pressed
2 *dry bay leaves, crumbled*
1¼ *lb. skinless, boneless*
  chicken breasts, cut into
  ¾-*inch cubes*
1½ *cups plain low-fat*
  yogurt
2 *Tbsp. minced cilantro*
1 *tsp. cumin seeds*
2½ *cups chicken broth*
1¾ *cups couscous*
½ *cup sliced green onions*
  (including tops)
Salt and pepper

In a nonreactive bowl, combine lemon juice, oil, wine, 6 minced garlic cloves, and bay leaves; reserve ¼ cup of marinade. Add chicken to remaining marinade, turning to coat. Cover and refrigerate for at least 30 minutes or up to 4 hours.

In a bowl, stir together yogurt, cilantro, cumin seeds, and the remaining minced garlic; cover and refrigerate for at least 15 minutes.

Lift chicken from marinade and drain briefly (discard marinade). Thread chicken equally on 8 metal skewers. Place chicken on a lightly greased grill 4 to 6 inches above a solid bed of medium-hot coals. Cook, basting with reserved marinade and turning as needed, until meat is lightly browned on outside and no longer pink in center (about 10 minutes); cut to test.

Meanwhile, in a 2- to 3-quart pan, bring broth to a boil over medium-high heat; stir in couscous. Cover, remove from heat, and let stand until liquid is absorbed (about 5 minutes). Stir in onion; season to taste with salt and pepper.

Makes 4 servings

Turkey-Pineapple Skewers

Turkey breast, skewered with fresh, juicy chunks of pineapple, makes a tropical-tasting entrée.

◆

PER SERVING: 274 calories, 37 g protein, 17 g carbohydrates, 5 g total fat, 103 mg cholesterol, 114 mg sodium

PREPARATION TIME: *15 min.*
MARINATING TIME: *1 hr.*
GRILLING TIME: *15 min.*

2½ lb. boned turkey breast, skinned
¼ cup butter or margarine
⅓ cup dry sherry
½ tsp. each paprika, ground sage, dry rosemary, and ground thyme
1 small pineapple

Rinse turkey, pat dry, and cut into 1½-inch chunks. Melt butter in a small pan; stir in sherry, paprika, sage, rosemary, and thyme; reserve ¼ cup mixture. Pour remaining butter mixture into a large bowl; add turkey and stir to coat. Cover and let stand for 1 hour.

Peel and core pineapple, then cut into 1½-inch chunks. Lift turkey from marinade and drain briefly (discard marinade). Thread turkey and pineapple chunks alternately on about 7 bamboo (see page 10) or metal skewers (each about 12 inches long), beginning and ending with turkey.

Place skewers on a lightly greased grill 4 to 6 inches above a solid bed of medium-hot coals. Cook, turning and basting with reserved marinade every few minutes until turkey is no longer pink (about 15 minutes total); cut to test.

Makes 6 servings

Skewered Turkey

Turkey tastes a bit like lamb when prepared with a mint-lime marinade and grilled.

◆

PER SERVING: *248 calories, 28 g protein, 6 g carbohydrates, 11 g total fat, 105 mg cholesterol, 115 mg sodium*

PREPARATION TIME: *15 min.*
MARINATING TIME: *1 hr.*
GRILLING TIME: *15 min.*

1 *turkey thigh (about 2 lb.),*
   skinned, boned
¼ *cup each salad oil and*
   dry white wine
¼ *cup mint jelly, melted*
¼ *tsp. grated lime zest*
1 *Tbsp. lime juice*
⅛ *tsp. pepper*

Rinse turkey thigh and pat dry. Cut meat into 1-inch chunks.

In a bowl, stir together oil, wine, jelly, lime zest, lime juice, and pepper; reserve ¼ cup marinade. Add meat to remaining marinade; turn to coat. Cover and refrigerate for at least 1 hour or until next day, stirring several times.

Lift meat from marinade and drain briefly (discard marinade). Thread meat equally on 4 metal skewers. Place skewers on a lightly greased grill 4 to 6 inches above a solid bed of medium coals. Cook, turning as needed, until turkey is well browned on all sides and no longer pink in center (about 15 minutes); cut to test. Baste several times with reserved marinade.

Makes 4 servings

Turkey Kebabs with Clam Sauce

Shellfish with fowl makes a lightened-up version of an old lobster-and-beef combination.

◆

PER SERVING: *450 calories, 144 g protein, 7 g carbohydrates, 26 g total fat, 134 mg cholesterol, 590 mg sodium*

PREPARATION TIME: *15 min.*
MARINATING TIME: *1 hr.*
GRILLING TIME: *12 min.*

1 *can (6½ oz.) minced clams*
2 *Tbsp. salad oil*
1 *Tbsp. ground sage*
½ *tsp. dry thyme leaves*
2 *lb. boneless turkey breast,*
   cut into 1½-inch cubes
24 *cherry tomatoes*
¾ *cups sour cream*
1 *can (4¼ oz.) chopped*
   ripe olives, drained
¼ *cup chopped green onions*
2 *crisp-cooked bacon*
   strips, crumbled

Drain clam juice into a bowl; reserve clams. To juice add oil, sage, thyme, and turkey; mix well. Cover and refrigerate at least 1 hour or up to 6 hours.

Lift turkey from marinade and drain briefly (discard marinade). Thread turkey and tomatoes alternately on 6 to 8 skewers. Place on a grill 4 to 6 inches above a solid bed of hot coals, turning to brown evenly until meat is white in center (9 to 12 minutes); cut to test.

Meanwhile, mix sour cream, reserved clams, olives, green onion, and bacon strips.

Place turkey on a platter; offer sauce to add to taste.

Makes 8 servings

FISH &
SEAFOOD

A hint of smoky flavor
from the barbecue enhances
just about any fresh fish or
shellfish. In this portion of the
book are kebab recipes featur-
ing everything from scallops
and shrimp to red snapper,
swordfish, and sea bass.

SCALLOPS & BACON SKEWERS, RECIPE ON PAGE 54

Scallops & Bacon Skewers

(PICTURED ON PAGE 52)

Scallops are teamed with bacon and grilled to perfection in this easy dish.

◆

PER SERVING: *309 calories, 29 g protein, 4 g carbohydrates, 19 g total fat, 92 mg cholesterol, 563 mg sodium*

PREPARATION TIME: *10 min.*
GRILLING TIME: *7 min.*

12 strips bacon
2 lb. scallops
6 Tbsp. butter or margarine,
   melted with 1 tsp. each
   chervil and paprika

Place separated bacon strips on a cold rack in a rimmed pan. Partially broil bacon about 6 inches from heat. Remove from heat; drain slightly on paper towels.

Wash scallops to remove any bits of shell or sand; pat dry with paper towels.

On each of 8 skewers, alternately thread bacon and scallops; bacon will form S-curves around scallops. Brush with flavored butter. Place scallops on a lightly greased grill 4 to 6 inches above a solid bed of hot coals. Cook, turning occasionally and basting with butter until bacon is crisp and scallops are cooked through (5 to 7 minutes); cut to test.

Makes 4 to 8 servings

Japanese Swimming Fish

Threaded on parallel bamboo skewers, these fish fillets look as if they're swimming.

◆

PER SERVING: *185 calories, 30 g protein, 4 g carbohydrates, 4 g total fat, 52 mg cholesterol, 863 mg sodium*

PREPARATION TIME: *30 min.*
MARINATING TIME: *10 min.*
GRILLING TIME: *10 min.*

4 *pieces firm-textured white*
  fish fillets such as red
  snapper, sea bass, or ling
  cod (1 to 1½ lb. total),
  cut ¾ to 1 inch thick
3 *Tbsp. soy sauce*
2 *Tbsp. mirin or cream*
  sherry
1 *Tbsp. lemon juice*
1½ *tsp. salad oil*

Rinse fish and pat dry. Thread 2 bamboo skewers (see page 10) lengthwise through each piece of fish, weaving skewers in and out of fish so fillets look slightly rippled; space skewers 1 inch apart.

In a small bowl, mix soy sauce, mirin, lemon juice, and oil; reserve 3 tablespoons. Brush the remaining soy mixture on both sides of fish pieces; let stand for 10 minutes.

Place fish on a well-greased grill 4 to 6 inches above a solid bed of hot coals. Cook, basting occasionally with reserved soy mixture and turning once, until fish flakes when prodded in thickest part (7 to 10 minutes).

Makes 4 servings

Garlicky Fish Skewers

This recipe from the Adriatic coast is topped with a chile-seasoned tomato relish.

◆

PER SERVING: 224 calories, 27 g protein, .38 g carbohydrates, 12 g total fat, 53 mg cholesterol, 121 mg sodium

PREPARATION TIME: *30 min.*
GRILLING TIME: *12 min.*

1 each *small fresh or canned hot red, green, and yellow chile*
2 *large tomatoes, peeled, diced*
1 *medium-size onion, finely chopped*
¼ *tsp. salt*
1 *tsp. sugar*
1 *Tbsp. red wine vinegar*
3 *Tbsp. olive oil*
2 *cloves garlic, minced or pressed*
¼ *tsp. pepper*
2 *lb. firm-textured fish steaks such as swordfish, halibut, turbot, or ling cod, skinned (if needed), cut into 1- by 1½-inch chunks*
Salt

Stem, seed, and finely chop chiles. Place chopped chiles in a nonreactive bowl and add tomatoes, onion, salt, sugar, and vinegar. Stir until well blended. Cover and refrigerate for at least 30 minutes or until next day.

In a bowl, combine oil, garlic, and pepper; add fish chunks and turn to coat. Thread fish chunks equally on 6 sturdy metal skewers.

Place skewers on a well-greased grill 4 to 6 inches above a solid bed of hot coals. Cook, turning several times, until fish flakes when prodded in thickest part (10 to 12 minutes). Season to taste with salt and serve with relish.

Makes 6 servings

Hawaiian Scallop Skewers

Alternate bacon, marinated scallops, and vegetables for these teriyaki-flavored skewers.

◆

PER SERVING: *285 calories, 30 g protein, 10 g carbohydrates, 13 g total fat, 62 mg cholesterol, 1,412 mg sodium*

PREPARATION TIME: *25 min.*
MARINATING TIME: *2 hr.*
GRILLING TIME: *7 min.*

16 scallops, each 1 to 1½
   inches in diameter
¼ cup soy sauce
1 Tbsp. each lemon juice,
   dry sherry, and salad oil
2 cloves garlic, minced
   or pressed
1 tsp. each minced fresh
   ginger and sugar
16 mushrooms, each 1 to
   1½ inches in diameter
4 slices bacon
2 small red bell peppers,
   seeded, cut into
   1½-inch squares

Rinse scallops to remove any bits of shell or sand.

In a nonreactive bowl, mix soy sauce, lemon juice, sherry, oil, garlic, ginger, and sugar; reserve ¼ cup. Add scallops and mushrooms to remaining marinade and turn to coat. Cover and refrigerate for 2 to 4 hours, turning several times.

Cook bacon in a wide frying pan over medium heat until it is partially cooked but still limp (about 3 minutes). Drain on paper towels. Cut each bacon slice into 4 pieces.

Lift scallops and mushrooms from marinade and drain briefly (discard marinade). Thread bacon pieces, scallops, mushrooms, and bell peppers alternately on bamboo skewers (see page 10). Place skewers on a well-greased grill 4 to 6 inches above a solid bed of hot coals. Cook, turning occasionally and basting several times with reserved marinade, until scallops are opaque throughout (5 to 7 minutes); cut to test.

Makes 4 servings

Mint-Flavored Shrimp

Chopped fresh mint enlivens the well-seasoned marinade for these grilled shrimp.

◆

PER SERVING: *374 calories, 25 g protein, 2 g carbohydrates, 29 g total fat, 186 mg cholesterol, 368 mg sodium*

PREPARATION TIME: *25 min.*
MARINATING TIME: *2 hr.*
GRILLING TIME: *5 min.*

¾ cup salad oil
1 Tbsp. finely chopped fresh
   mint or 1 Tbsp. dry mint,
   crumbled
1 Tbsp. white wine vinegar
1 tsp. each chili powder
   and dry basil
½ tsp. salt
¼ tsp. pepper
1 clove garlic, minced
   or pressed
2 lb. medium-size raw
   shrimp (30 to 32 per lb.),
   shelled, deveined

In a large nonreactive bowl, stir together oil, mint, vinegar, chili powder, basil, salt, pepper, and garlic; reserve ⅓ cup. Add shrimp to remaining marinade and stir to coat. Cover and refrigerate for 2 to 4 hours.

Lift shrimp from marinade and drain briefly (discard marinade). Thread about 5 shrimp on a pair of bamboo (see page 10) or thin metal skewers, aligning skewers parallel so shrimp lie flat. Repeat with remaining shrimp. Place shrimp on a well-greased grill 4 to 6 inches above a solid bed of hot coals. Cook, basting with reserved marinade and turning once, until shrimp turn pink (3 to 5 minutes).

Makes 6 servings

Prawns & Tomatoes
with Basil Oil

Succulent prawns need little adornment to make a dramatic presentation.

◆

PER SERVING: *270 calories, 23 g protein, 10 g carbohydrates, 16 g total fat, 159 mg cholesterol, 171 mg sodium*

PREPARATION TIME: *15 min.*
GRILLING TIME: *6 min.*

*1 to 1¼ lb. colossal (10
to 15 per lb.) or extra-
colossal prawns (8 to 10
per lb.)*
¼ cup extra-virgin olive oil
*1 clove garlic, minced
or pressed*
*2 Tbsp. minced fresh basil
or 1 tsp. dry basil*
*3 large firm-ripe tomatoes,
cored, cut crosswise into
½-inch-thick slices*
*4 large romaine leaves,
washed, crisped*
Salt and pepper
Fresh basil sprigs (optional)

Peel and devein prawns. Thread equal portions of prawns on each of 4 skewers. Mix the oil, garlic, and basil. Brush prawns and tomatoes with basil oil.

Place prawns and tomatoes on a grill 4 to 6 inches above a solid bed of hot coals. Cook, brushing tomatoes and prawns with basil oil, turning them once, until prawns are just opaque in thickest part and tomatoes are hot (about 6 minutes total for both); cut to test.

Place 1 romaine leaf on each of 4 dinner plates. Place tomatoes on romaine; set prawns alongside. Drizzle prawns and tomatoes with remaining basil oil. Add salt and pepper to taste. Garnish with basil sprigs.

Makes 4 servings

Scallops with
Ginger-Lime Sauce

*S*erve grilled scallops in a pale green sauce sparked with fresh ginger.

♦

PER SERVING: *442 calories, 41 g protein, 6 g carbohydrates, 31 g total fat, 141 mg cholesterol, 499 mg sodium*

PREPARATION TIME: *30 min.*
GRILLING TIME: *7 min.*

½ cup each *dry white wine
 and chicken broth*
2 Tbsp. *minced shallots
 or onion*
1 tsp. *grated fresh ginger*
¼ tsp. *grated lime zest*
½ cup *whipping cream*
¼ cup *unsalted butter*
1½ lb. *scallops, each 1 to
 1½ inches in diameter*
¼ cup *butter or margarine,
 melted*

In a wide frying pan, combine wine, chicken broth, shallots, ginger, and lime zest. Bring to a boil over high heat; continue to boil, uncovered, until reduced by half. Stir in cream and boil, uncovered, until reduced to ¾ cup. Reduce heat to medium and add butter all in one chunk; stir constantly until butter is completely blended into sauce. To keep sauce warm for up to 2 hours, pour into a 2-cup glass measure set in hot-to-touch water. Stir occasionally and replace water as needed.

Wash scallops to remove any bits of shell or sand; pat dry with paper towels.

Thread scallops on bamboo skewers (see page 10), piercing them horizontally (through their diameter) so they lie flat. Brush with butter. Place scallops on a well-greased grill 4 to 6 inches above a solid bed of hot coals. Cook, turning once, until scallops are opaque throughout (5 to 7 minutes); cut to test.

Lay scallops in sauce on a warm platter.

Makes 4 servings

Index